Jesus: who did he think he was?

Exploring the meaning behind his names

H. J. RICHARDS

Kevin Mayhew

First published in 2000 by
KEVIN MAYHEW LTD
Buxhall
Stowmarket
Suffolk IP14 3BW

© 2000 H. J. Richards

The right of H. J. Richards to be identified
as the author of this work has been asserted
by him in accordance with the Copyright,
Designs and Patents Act 1988.

All rights reserved.
No part of this publication may be reproduced,
stored in a retrieval system, or transmitted,
in any form or by any means, electronic, mechanical,
photocopying, recording or otherwise, without the
prior written permission of the publisher.

0 1 2 3 4 5 6 7 8 9

ISBN 1 84003 658 3
Catalogue No 1500398

Cover design by Jonathan Stroulger
Edited by Elizabeth Bates
Typesetting by Louise Selfe
Printed and bound in Great Britain

Contents

Introduction	5
Section One	
1. God	11
2. Lord	15
3. Word of God	18
4. Son of God	20
Section Two	
1. Son of Man	27
2. Messiah-Christ	31
3. Suffering Servant	34
4. Saviour	37
5. Holy One of God	40
6. Chosen – Elect	42
7. Mediator	44
8. Prophet	47
9. Second Adam – Image of God	49
10. Conclusion	51
Acknowledgements	54

INTRODUCTION

I suppose that it is not the best of all selling points to turn the title of a book into a question, and then spend the rest of the book saying, 'I don't know the answer'. But the fact is that even scholars who have devoted their lives to studying the titles given to Jesus in the New Testament have only been able to come up with the most hesitant of answers to that question.

There is no problem about who Jesus' *disciples* thought he was: they have given us a wide spectrum of a dozen or more titles to express their aspirations and convictions. We shall, of course, ask the question whether Jesus himself would have agreed with the implications behind these titles, as long as it is understood that this is a different cup of tea. Of which, however, we might get a little taste in passing.

In a recent publication of excerpts from his diary, God has revealed some of his most private thoughts:

AD 26, *3 April*
I've warmed strongly to a new arrival in Galilee –
   a carpenter named Jesus.
His name means 'Saviour'.
I can just see this man making the breakthrough
   which could save the human race.
He's young yet, and has a lot to learn.
But he's beginning to show people
   what it could mean to say
   that human beings are destined to be
   my 'sons and daughters',
   filled with my godly Spirit as he is.
When he went down to the Jordan
   to join John the Baptiser,
I said to myself, 'Yes, this *is* my son.'

AD 28, 23 *March*
It's a sheer joy to see Jesus
    handling his thick-headed disciples
    with such patience and tolerance.
Especially Peter, the thickest of the lot.
His attitude reflects exactly
    the amazing grace
    with which I've patiently tolerated
    the human race over these millennia.
This man is like a window into me.
To see him is to see me, without distortion.
You could say that, for all my mystery,
    I am Jesus-shaped.
He is the whole truth about me,
    being lived-out in the life of an ordinary human being.

AD 30, *4 April*
Jesus' preferential option for the poor
    is beginning to arouse opposition.
Right from the outset,
    he's identified himself with the disadvantaged,
    the outcasts, the losers, the marginalised, the 'heretics' –
    further evidence of how, day by day,
    he becomes more and more like me.

AD 30, *6 April*
The opposition to Jesus has grown.
We're clearly close to flashpoint.
Tonight he brought his closest followers together
    for the Passover meal.
At the traditional breaking of the bread,
    he spoke of his body soon to be broken in death.
And he repeated these forebodings
    at the end of the meal,
    when he spoke of his blood being poured out
    as freely as the last cup of wine.

The police later picked him up.
My son, my son,
   why do you think I've forsaken you?
Believe me, I'm closer to you than ever.
And you to me.

AD 30, *7 April*
They killed him today, Friday.
A cruel and lingering death, but he went like a lamb.
I suppose it was inevitable.
Given what my world has become
   over these thousands of years,
   it was bound to be at cross purposes
   with those who share my priorities,
   and show themselves to be true children of mine.
Do I regard it as a tragedy?
How could I regard it as anything else?
If sparrows don't fall to the ground
   without it tearing my heart out,
   what should I say
   about the death of this son of mine?
Yet I refuse to think of it as an unmitigated disaster.
This won't be the end of the Jesus story.
He has not died into nothing.
He has died into me.

AD 30, *9 April*
Jesus' friends are already experiencing him
   as being closer to them now
   than he ever was in his lifetime.
His women friends in particular.
Killing him has made him live.
So that when people ask them where Jesus is now,
   they no longer point to the cemetery
   as they were doing last Friday.
They point to their own community,

in which Jesus is marvellously embodied
in a new way.
It's as if his death has allowed the godly Spirit
with which he was filled
to pour out into the wide world.
Those who live in that Spirit
are already in my presence,
as Jesus always was,
and still is.

AD 30, *18 June*
Not two months after he died,
Jesus' followers had already grown
to three thousand.
This week they number five thousand.
This could be the beginning of something big.

> H. J. Richards, *God's Diary*, Columba Press, 1991

Even in these short excerpts, there are references to as many as nine of the titles given to Jesus: Son of God, Word of God, Window into God, Servant of God, Lamb of God, Image of God, Saviour, New Adam, Spirit-filled. All of them can be found in the writings of the first disciples of Jesus. What exactly did they mean? Would Jesus have approved? And if he had, what exactly did these titles mean for him?

In trying to answer these questions, I am thinking of the many GCSE and A-level students whom I have tried to steer through the labyrinths of Old Testament and New Testament theology, especially in the area of Christology and the Christian Understanding of God. I am hoping that what follows may help their younger brothers and sisters prepare for their exams, which (I am delighted to see) will still be based on New Testament options in all three of the new A-level syllabuses (AQA, Edexel and OCR) now being introduced.

Parish study groups, and those studying for the newly restored Roman Catholic order of the diaconate, may also find the book useful. Obviously they will need to read far more widely than these few pages, and find out from the biblical scholars themselves how they arrived at their conclusions. All I have provided here is what I hope may be a useful summary of their findings.

Section One
1. GOD

Text ascribed to Thomas Aquinas, trans. G. M. Hopkins
Music: Gregory Murray. © 1976 Kevin Mayhew Ltd

God-head here in hid - ing, whom I do a-dore.

As Christians, we take what is known as the 'divinity' of Jesus so easily for granted ('God the Father, God the Son', 'God from God, true God from true God') that it comes as something of a shock to discover that there is no text in the New Testament where Jesus ever gives himself that title ('Oh, by the way, I am Almighty God').

On the contrary. There are a dozen texts where he says the very opposite. For example:

> 'Good Master,' a hopeful disciple begins, and Jesus cuts him short: 'Why do you call *me* good? Only *one* is good – God.' (Mark 10:18)

> In the Temptation scene, the devil says, 'Worship me, and I will give you all the kingdoms of the world.' The reply of Jesus is uncompromising: 'You must worship God *only*, no one else.' (Luke 4:8)

> When he is at his last gasp on the Cross, Jesus cries out: 'My God, my God, why have you forsaken me?' (Matthew 27:46). How could *God* say that?

> Even the evangelist, John, who is otherwise very keen on stressing the divinity of Jesus, represents him as saying: 'If you really loved me, you would be glad that I am going to God, my Father, because the Father is *greater than I.*' (John 14:28)

'This is eternal life,' says the Jesus of John's Gospel. 'To know the *one* God, and him whom that one God has sent, Jesus Christ'; and the two are distinct from each other. (John 17:3)

Paul puts it most pithily: 'For us, there is *one* God, the Father from whom all things come – and one Lord Jesus Christ.' (1 Corinthians 8:6)

But not only did Jesus himself never claim that he was God. None of his disciples got anywhere near claiming that – except in two rather obscure texts. At the end of St John's Gospel, the shocked disciple Thomas falls on his knees before the risen Christ to say:

My Lord and my God (John 20:28),

but even that is only a quotation of a phrase which occurs in numerous Psalms. And in the Epistle to the Hebrews, Christ is addressed in the words:

Your throne, O God, stands for ever (Hebrews 1:8),

but this also is an explicit quotation from the Book of Psalms. And then, of course, there is the famous opening line of John's Gospel:

In the beginning was the Word, and the Word was with God, and the Word *was* God (John 1:1),

but the word here translated as 'God' should more accurately be 'divine' (the Greek word is *theos*, not *ho theos*), and might be better translated:

'and what God was, the Word was'.

Why does the New Testament show such reluctance to give Jesus the title we so easily give him? The answer is simple. In biblical usage, 'God' is the title of the Father, and no one has ever wanted to claim that Jesus was God the Father. The Bible will happily give Jesus a dozen different divine titles, but they are always 'The *x* of God' or 'The *y* of God'; never 'God', full stop. Jesus is the *Son* of God, showing the world what it means to have God as a father; the *Word* of God, opening out the meaning of the letters G. O. D; the *Servant* of God, doing not his own will but God's; the *Prophet* of God, acting as the very mouthpiece of God; the *Chosen* of God, selected from all others as God's favourite or darling; the *Image* or *Reflection* of God, in whom one can see what the mysterious God might look like in human terms; the *Way* to God, whose path we must tread in order to reach God; and so on. But 'God' remains the exclusive title of the Father, who will always remain *the* impenetrable mystery. Christians are simply those who claim to know and have access to that mystery in the life of Jesus.

A final footnote: If God (in order to be God) has to remain a mystery, then the only way in which we can speak of Jesus is indirectly, by means of metaphors. 'Son of God' is a metaphor, as also are the terms 'Word', 'Servant', 'Prophet', 'Way', etc. We ought not to be surprised, therefore, if the Bible calls not only Jesus such a metaphor, but the rest of the human race too!

> *You* must be perfect (says Jesus to his disciples), just as your heavenly Father is perfect. (Matthew 5:48)
>
> We are *all of us*, even now, the children of God (says St John) and called eventually to be just like God, when we see him as he is. (1 John 3:2)
>
> We are called to become the very *images* of Christ (says Paul), as younger brothers and sisters of his. (Romans 8:29)
>
> *All* of us (says Peter, or one of his spokesmen in the New Testament) are called to share in the very being of God. (1 Peter 1:4)

St Irenaeus, the second-century theologian, has echoed these lively quotations in the saying for which he has become famous:

The Glory of God is revealed in human beings who are fully alive.

What a challenge!

Questions for discussion

- 'I've got no time for a Jesus who is *only* a member of the human race.'
  'I've got no time for a Jesus who is *not* a member of the human race.'
  Which of these two statements expresses your view? Explain why.

- Who is/was Jesus? Is 'God' the least confusing answer, or the most?

2. LORD

Text unknown
Music unknown, arr. Adrian Vernon Fish
Arrangement © 1994 Kevin Mayhew Ltd

He is Lord, he is Lord.

Alongside the title 'God', and not strongly distinct from it, is the title 'Lord'. Behind it lies quite a complicated history.

According to the Book of Exodus, God revealed his personal name to Moses at Mount Sinai. The name is 'Yahweh' (see Exodus 3:14). But this name, on closer inspection, turns out to be rather less revealing than Moses was expecting. In full, the words *Yahweh asher yahweh* mean no more than 'He is *who* he is' – in short, 'Mind your own business!'

On the other hand, this curt reply could be *the* revelation of all time. God refuses to give his name, not because he doesn't want to, but because he can't. When Moses asks, 'Who are you, so that we can index you among other names?', God replies, 'No name or title can capture what I am. I am who I am, the Mystery beyond all definition or classification.'

Certainly that is the way the Jews eventually understood this text. In the course of their history, this enigmatic reply of God in its abbreviated form (*Yahweh* – 'He is') took on such an aura of mystery, that they refused to pronounce it. Every time it occurred in their sacred texts, they substituted the word *Adonay*, meaning 'Lord'. And to remind themselves to say 'Adonay' instead of 'Yahweh', they inserted the vowels *a o a* into the consonants J H V H – which is why people unaware of this pronounced the name 'Jahovah', unaware that no Jew ever called God that. (In parenthesis, the famous Bible translator of the 50s, Ronald Knox, also refused to use the name 'Yahweh', not out of reverence but because, for him, they formed 'the ugliest collection of consonants and vowels ever invented – no wonder the Jews kept it dark'. When I acted as one of his editors, he wrote to say that he would have no objection to any further changes being made to his translation after he died. 'I will not turn in my grahweh,' he told me, 'except over Yahweh.')

All the first translations of the Old Testament respected this Jewish tradition, and that is why the name 'Yahweh' is always represented by 'Kyrios' in the Greek, by 'Dominus' in the Latin, and by 'the Lord' in the English versions. Only English versions have left a clue that a whole history lies behind this usage – by printing all four letters of the name in capitals: L O R D. This means, of course, that in hundreds of cases, the word 'Lord' that we read in the Old Testament stands for the divine name 'Yahweh'.

> The Lord is my shepherd. (Psalm 23)
>
> Taste and see that the Lord is good. (Psalm 34)
>
> Out of the depths I cry to thee, O Lord. (Psalm 130), and so on.

When we turn to the New Testament, and find that the title of 'Lord' is used about Jesus, is it this strong sense of divinity that we are meant to read into it? In many case, the answer is obviously 'yes'.

> How is it that the mother of my *Lord* should come to me? (Luke 1:43)
>
> Today is born for you a Saviour, who is Christ the *Lord*. (Luke 2:11)
>
> *Lord*, to whom should we go? You have the words of eternal life. (John 6:68)

This is particularly the case after the Resurrection. In Acts 2:36 the Resurrection is referred to as the action in which the Jesus whom his enemies had crucified became *Lord*. In Philippians 2:9 Jesus is said to possess *the* name above all others, which is *Lord*. In Romans 10:9 the original Christian creed is said to consist of the three words 'Jesus is *Lord*'. And by the time we reach the letters of Paul, the words 'Christ our *Lord*' has become a refrain.

The question, of course, must be asked: Does this usage date back to Jesus' lifetime? Did people give him that title then? And if they did, did Jesus accept it?

It is interesting that, although Matthew, Luke and John recorded Jesus being addressed as 'Lord' over and over again, in the earliest Gospel of Mark this happens only once. Is it the case that the historical Jesus was never actually addressed in this way? And if he was (as Matthew, Luke and John suggest), have we any way of knowing whether, in the context, it meant anything more than 'Sir' or 'Mister'? Even today, that is all it means in Hebrew (*Adon* Barak), or Greek (*Kyrios* Stafulos) or Spanish (*Don* Carlos). When I was a student in Rome, my title at the university was *Dominus Richards*. No one thought I was divine!

Questions for discussion

- What overtones, attractive or unattractive, does the title 'Lord' have for you?

- When you come across the title 'Lord' in prayers or hymns, do you think of God the Father or of Jesus? Does it matter?

3. WORD OF GOD

Text and music attributed to John Francis Wade
Trans. Frederick Oakeley

Word of the Fa - ther, now in flesh ap - pear - ing.

As a title of Jesus, this is to be found only in the opening lines of John's Gospel, though there are echoes of it in the opening lines of his Epistle (see 1 John 1:1). But when John uses it, he presumes that his readers are familiar enough with the Old Testament to appreciate that the theme of 'the Word' dominates the whole Bible.

The very first image in the first lines of the first book of the Bible is that of God speaking his Word. 'In the beginning, God created the heavens and the earth'. How? Listen:

> God spoke the Word, 'Let there be light', and there was light.
> God spoke the Word, 'Let there be a firmament', and there was.
> God spoke the Word, 'Let dry land appear', and it did.
> God spoke the Word, 'Let the earth produce living creatures of all kinds', and it did.
> God spoke the Word, 'Let us make human beings, male and female, in our own image and likeness', and there were humans.

The whole of creation is here being presented as the product of God's Word. In other words, the whole of creation speaks of God to those who have ears to hear.

And then the Old Testament continues the story, with the same Word of God coming to Abraham, promising that his people will be God's own. And to Moses, in order to give this people a Law to live by:

> The Word is not in the heavens or overseas; it is close to you. (Deuteronomy 30:14)

And then to a whole line of prophets, in order to guide and comfort this people. God's Spirit (or Breath) passes though the lips of these men, so that what issues is no longer the word of Isaiah or Jeremiah or Ezekiel, but the Word of God: 'Now hear the Word of the Lord.'

This is the background against which the prologue to John's Gospel was written. For John, the whole long history of God speaking his Word, that is to say, of revealing himself more and more clearly to his world and to his people, come to a climax in Jesus of Nazareth:

> In the beginning was the Word . . .
> and the Word was made flesh,
> embodied in the life of a human being. (John 1:1-14)

In Jesus, says John, we can read God like a book. He is the Truth about God. He is the last word on God. There is nothing more to add.

An echo of this title of Jesus appears in the Synoptic Gospel accounts of the Transfiguration, in which a voice from heaven proclaims, 'This is my Son; *listen* to him' (Mark 9:7). But John's image of the divine voice embodied in the life of a human being is far stronger, and provides a powerful addition to the list of titles given to Jesus by his disciples.

Questions for discussion

- List some of the implications of the term 'word', and ask whether they help you understand what it means to call Jesus the Word of *God*.

- We give the name 'Word of God' to both Jesus and the Bible. Why?

4. SON OF GOD

Music: H. J. Richards, *The Gospel in Song*
© Kevin Mayhew Ltd, 1983

The Son of God, that was his name.

To understand this title of Jesus, it would be useful to consider and compare some texts like the following:

> The *sons* of God came to present themselves before Yahweh, and Satan was among them. (Job 1:6)
>
> (God says): Israel is my firstborn *son*. (Exodus 4:22)
>
> (God says to David): I will raise up your son (Solomon) after you; I will be his Father, and he will be my *son*. (2 Samuel 7:12)
>
> Blessed are the peacemakers, for they shall be called the *sons* of God. (Matthew 5:9)
>
> (The long inverse genealogy of Jesus ends with the words): Enosh was the son of Seth, Seth was the son of Adam, and Adam was the *son* of God. (Luke 3:38)

If the title 'Son of God' can be applied across such a wide spectrum, there is obviously some ambiguity about it. Clearly it is a metaphor, since God is not a father in the ordinary sense of the word. Yet he *is* something like a father, and therefore anyone who somehow shares in his life can be called his son, whether it is the *angels* who are sent out like messengers from his household (Job), or the *Israelite people* among whom he was believed to dwell (Exodus), or the *king* who was appointed to sum up the whole nation before

God (2 Samuel), or the *virtuous man* who reflects all the qualities of God, like father like son (Matthew), or indeed any *Adam* and Eve who acknowledge God as their creator (Luke).

This means, of course, that when Jesus is given this title in the New Testament, he is being described, superlatively, as the Messenger of God, the True Israel, the new David, the Just and Virtuous Man, the Brother of all the sons and daughters of Adam.

Strangely, in spite of this wide spread of meaning, the title is not given to Jesus all that easily in the Gospels. True, in the Temptation scene in the opening pages, Satan assumes that Jesus *is* Son of God, and tries to discover what sort of a son this might be ('If you *are* the Son of God, then . . .'). And again, half-way through the Gospels, in the Transfiguration scene, the Voice from heaven acclaims him ('You *are* the Son of God'). But the title is almost totally absent from Jesus' public ministry as told by Matthew, Mark and Luke, except in the voice of people possessed by Satan. And when these begin to give him that title because of his healing powers, he seems strangely embarrassed by it (see Mark 3:12). Even when Peter merrily gives him the title in the famous Confession scene, Jesus forbids it, and shortly after accuses even Peter of being a tool of Satan (Mark 8:27-33). And finally, in the trial before the Sanhedrim, where he is charged with assuming this title for himself, '*Are* you the Son of God?' his reply (according to Matthew and Luke) is, 'You have said it'. Many translations take this to mean, 'You bet!' – but they are sadly wrong. It means, 'That's *your* word, Caiaphas. *My* word is "Son of Man"'. It is a total repudiation of the title. (In parenthesis, it has to be said that in Mark's telling of this story Jesus does actually accept the title. But he has his own theological reason for doing so. According to Mark, it is only in his passion and death that Jesus finally makes it clear what being God's Son entails in a world such as ours).

It is only in the last of the four Gospels, John, that there is no hesitation or embarrassment about using the title. From Chapter 1 ('The *only Son* of the Father') down to Chapter 20 ('These things have been written so that you may believe that Jesus is the *Son of God'),* the title occurs 35 times, most often on Jesus' own lips. He is described quite simply as *the* Son, full stop. And by the time we get to Paul, the title has become so common that it is used another 42 times.

We are, then, again left in a quandary. It is obvious that Jesus saw God as his Father, and therefore he would have no difficulty about seeing his relationship to God as sonship. But did he ever claim to be Son with a capital S, as a specific *title*? Did he ever describe himself as *the* Son, the only, unique? There would have been very good reasons not to, because this was one of the titles of the expected Messiah, the new David, and that is a title about which he was very ambiguous, as we shall see below.

Certainly all his followers happily look up to him as *the* Son of God *par excellence*, the Model of sonship, showing to an eminent degree what is involved in claiming that God is our Father. Of all the sons and daughters of God, he is the ideal, the firstborn as it were, in whom one can see what the invisible Father must be like.

And yet all of us are called to be that as well, as we become conformed to his image, says Paul (Romans 8:29). Indeed, the ideal Christian prayer is to call God what Jesus called him, 'Abba, Father' (Galatians 4:6). Isn't that precisely what Jesus himself meant when he referred to God so inclusively as 'my Father and your Father'? (See John 20:17.) 'What love God has shown in calling *us also* his sons, because that is what we are.' (1 John 3:1)

Questions for discussion

- We call Jesus 'Son of God' when we think of God as 'Father'. What should we call Jesus when we use other metaphors about God – Creator, Light, Rock, Husband, Shepherd, Lord?

- Do you see 'Son of God' as a very strong title of Jesus, or a weak one?

John's Gospel: A footnote

The titles given to Jesus in the Gospel of John require a separate entry: they are in a category of their own. A friend of mine once compared reading John's Gospel to booking a Tube ticket from Paddington to Charing Cross, and minutes later finding oneself in outer space. Rather disconcerting for the ordinary commuter, but what a bonus for anyone keen on space travel!

The titles John gives Jesus are space-titles. They express, not what Jesus was, but (as the Scripture scholar William Barclay puts it) 'what Jesus *becomes* to someone who has known him for a very long time'. The poet Robert Browning realised this long before the Scripture scholars did, and pictured the dying John explaining how his Gospel should be read:

> What first were guessed as points, I now knew stars,
> And named them in the Gospel I have writ.
> *A Death in the Desert*, lines 174-5

In other words, if you only want the points, you must go to a historian. John has taken a space-flight, and discovered that the points a historian makes are (in this case) stars, and insists on naming them, and exploring them, and explaining them. The Jesus he presents, and the titles with which he invests him, are not snapshots taken fifty years earlier. They are the end result of decades of exploration. For John, Jesus has become *the* Light that illumines our path through the darkness surrounding us (John 8:12); *the* Truth about the God we know only fitfully (14:6); *the* Life that overcomes the death constantly threatening us (11:25); *the* Way that leads to the unfathomable mystery of God (14:6); *the* Shepherd who leads God's flock so faithfully that he will put his own life on the line for them (10:11); *the* Bread without which we would die in our desert journey to the Land promised to us (6:35); *the* Door through which we enter into the presence of God (10:7).

John presents Jesus in these absolute terms because that is what

Jesus now means for him. He writes his Gospel to ask whether he means that for his readers too.

Which is not to say that these titles are exclusive. All Christians are called to be other Christs. The 'Imitation of Christ' means precisely that what Jesus was, his followers are invited to be too. What me, the light by which others can find their way to God? Yes, of course. 'You are the light of the world' (Matthew 5:14). What *me*, the truth about God, open to the scrutiny of all those who are searching? Yes of course: 'The truth lives *in us* and will be with us for ever' (1 John 1:2). What *me*, the life that stands as a countersign to the world's culture of death? Yes, of course: 'I give eternal life to *all* who follow me' (John 10:28); What *me*, the way on which others may come to God? Yes of course: '*Anyone* who claims to live in God must walk in the way of Jesus' (1 John 2:6). What *me*, the shepherd responsible for the health and safety of God's people? Yes, of course: '*You*, the disciple, must now tend and feed my sheep' (John 21:16-17). What *me*, the bread that has to be broken to feed the world? Yes, of course: 'I was hungry and *you* gave me food' (Matthew 25:35). What *me*, the door that must remain ever open for those who are looking for their home? Yes, of course: 'The door of faith has been opened to the pagans' through the preaching of Jesus' *disciples* (Acts 14:27).

If I was told that, along with my Desert Island Discs, I could choose only one of the four Gospels to take with me, it would have to be John's. I shall have words with him, when we finally meet, about the virulent anti-Semitism which keeps blurring what he has to say, and perhaps he will take me back to the turmoil of the first century and ask me whether at that time I could have done any better. But even this lapse cannot dim his vision of Jesus, which continues to inspire me like no other. Through John, Jesus has become for me the Word, whose every twist and turn speaks to me of God. I have to watch this Word like a hawk, or (with John) like an eagle.

Perhaps it would be useful, before passing on to less 'heavy-weight' titles of Jesus, to make a short summary of what I have tried to say so far, lest it be thought that I am trying to water down the Christian message in order to make it easier to swallow. All I am trying to do is to remain faithful to the original Christian Good News of 'incarnation'.

To believe in 'incarnation' is to believe that the mysterious God, whom people tend to look for up there, in the beyond, in the infinite distance, is to be found down here, close, in something as ordinary as the life of a human being, *in carne*, in human flesh and blood.

This takes some believing! Far easier to believe in an ethereal otherwordly Being out there. But to claim that the invisible mystery of God is present, and at work, and clearly revealed in the life of an ordinary human being . . . no wonder the Romans called the first Christians 'atheists!'

For us Christians (I can't speak for other believers in God), the *human* is adequate to express the divine. When we speak of the divinity of Jesus, we are not trying to add something on top of his humanity. The divine and the human in Jesus do not make two. The divinity that we ascribe to him is not separable from his humanity. We call him 'Son of God' because he is the *Man* that he is, not because of something extra. Christians are those who claim to know what God is like by looking at the man Jesus. Not at something beyond him, or behind him, but only at the man. It is in this utterly human life that we claim to see, undistorted, the face of God.

SECTION TWO

1. SON OF MAN

Text: Michael Cockett
Music: Sister Madeleine. © 1978 Kevin Mayhew Ltd

The Son of Man has no place to lie down.

I have called the titles given to Jesus in the first part of this book 'heavyweight.' The ones that follow in this part are less extraordinary, but no less complex.

Take the first of these titles, 'Son of Man', which occurs 80 times in the Gospels, and with only two or three exceptions nowhere else in the New Testament. What does it mean to most readers of the New Testament? What particular aspect of Jesus does it emphasise?

Since the title is found only in the Gospels (never in St Paul), and only ever on Jesus' own lips (no one else's), it is pretty certain that it is a genuine title used by Jesus about himself, and not something imposed on Jesus by others. But this does not solve the question of what precisely he meant by using that title, since the Old Testament from which he borrowed it gives it four quite different meanings!

- The Hebrew language uses the words 'son of' when it wants to describe something as belonging to a certain category. We do it ourselves when we call someone 'a son of the soil', or 'a son of a gun', or 'a son of a bitch'. At this level, 'son of man' means nothing more than someone belonging to the category of man, a human being. The Old Testament has plenty of examples of this usage, for example in the parallel lines of Psalm 8:
    What is man that God should take notice of him,
    or the son of man that God should care about him?

- The prophet Ezekiel gave a clever twist to the title by comparing it to his own name Yehezk-el, which means 'God is strong'. 'Which is exactly what I'm *not!*' says the prophet, and keeps on and on referring to himself as 'Son of Man' – 93 times in total.

For him, the words clearly mean 'Poor old Ezekiel' – feeble, weak, impotent, fragile, the Suffering Servant.

- 450 years later, the Book of Daniel gave the title a twist in the opposite direction (Daniel 7:13). Among the many allegories he wove to describe the politics of his day, he imagines four nightmare beasts – a winged lion, a ravenous bear, a ferocious leopard, and a terrifying creature with iron teeth and ten horns. He tells us exactly what these represent: the four great empires which had succeeded each other in the Middle East up to his time – the Babylonians, the Medes, the Persians, and the Greek Empire of the successors of Alexander the Great. But he concludes the horrific vision with the wild hope that all these four evil empires will be replaced by (no longer a bestial figure, but) a humane one, the Son of Man, who *ascends* to heaven to be crowned as emperor by God himself. At the end of the chapter (7:27) he explains the details of the allegory: the pagan empires will be replaced by the Martyred Israel, the People of God.

- Finally we come to the apocalyptic literature which grew up in the turmoil of the last centuries BC. This literature seized upon Daniel's metaphor, and turned it into a way of speaking about God himself. The world would soon be ruled, no longer by these earthly powers, but by an individual heavenly figure, pre-existent and superhuman, scarcely distinct from God himself, who would *descend* from heaven to establish the Kingdom of God which mere humans had again and again failed to achieve. By this stage, the lower-case son of man had become the capital Son of capital Man, bearing a title paradoxically more divine than any mere son of God!

In which of these four senses is the title used on the many occasions that it comes up in the New Testament? The answer is, on different occasions, all four!

- There are texts in the Gospel where the words are totally neutral, and merely a third person circumlocution for the first person 'I'. 'Who do people say the Son of Man is?' asks Jesus in Matthew 16:13. The parallel texts in Mark and Luke have simply, 'Who do people say I am?' There are many places in the Gospels where this happens. Indeed, we still have the usage in English ('One feels the need to be on one's own'), though the Hebrew usage is rather less highbrow.

- There are other texts where the words 'Son of Man' have clear overtones of suffering, as in Ezekiel:
  'The Son of Man has nowhere to lay his head.' (Luke 9:58)
  'The Son of Man (it is written) will be betrayed into the hands of sinners.' (Mark 14:21)

- Finally there are many texts where the 'Son of Man' is a figure of such apocalyptic glory that Jesus seems to be talking about a third party, not himself. For instance:
  'Everyone who acknowledges me before men,
  the Son of Man will acknowledge him before
  the angels of God.' (Luke 12:8)

It should be clear from this small sample of texts what the words 'Son of Man' meant to the evangelists. They have capitalised on the ambiguity of the title, and after the death and resurrection of Jesus have attributed all four meanings to him. What is not clear is what the title meant to Jesus himself in his lifetime. A few scholars think that Jesus deliberately chose this ambiguous title in order to express his claim to be the Messiah, but without the militaristic overtones of the word 'Messiah'. Most scholars however are of the opinion that this high meaning of the title dates back to the early Christian community, not to Jesus himself. He himself, in using the words, probably meant no more than 'I'. The Jewish scholar Geza Vermes has found dozens of examples of rabbis in Jesus' own time using the term about themselves. In which case the words do not constitute a title at all, and they are quite unusable as an indication of who Jesus thought he was. All they tell us is what his disciples concluded he was.

Questions for Discussion

- What overtones do the words 'Son of Man' have for you when you come across them in the Gospels?

- Is this Gospel title of Jesus so complex and ambiguous that it is now quite untranslatable? Give reasons for and against.

2. MESSIAH-CHRIST

Text: Charles Wesley
Music adapted from Mendelssohn by W. H. Cummings

'Christ is born in Beth - le - hem.'

'Messiah' is the Hebrew word for 'anointed'. It translates into Greek as 'Christos'. Anointing with oil was the ceremony by which prophets, priests and kings were given their appointment in the Old Testament. This means that there were dozens of messiahs through Israelite history – not to mention English history, where our own kings and queens have been 'christed' in the same fashion.

It was only when the monarchy came to an end among the Jews, and they longed for *the* ideal king who would restore their position among the other world powers, that the title acquired as it were a capital M, and came to refer to the hoped-for future Liberator. Jeremiah 30:9 looks forward to a future when God will bring salvation under another David.

Ezekiel 34:3 promises that a future Shepherd – a new David – will feed his people Israel. Hosea 3:5 sees an ideal future, in which Israel will return to David their king.

It was in the light of this future hope that a number of Psalms, originally written for the coronation of kings x, y and z, were resurrected and reapplied to this future King-Messiah-Christ:

> Why do the nations imagine a vain thing against the Lord and his Anointed – his Christ? (Psalm 2:1)

> God, give your own justice to the King . . .
> In his days virtue will flourish,
> and universal peace till the moon is no more. (Psalm 72:1-7)

> The oracle of Yahweh to my Lord, the King:
> Sit at my right, with your enemies as your footstool. (Psalm 110:1)

The New Testament announces that these Old Testament hopes were fulfilled in Jesus of Nazareth. The announcement is made rather hesitantly in Mark and Matthew; more strongly in Luke 2:11 ('This day in the town of David a Saviour is born, who is *Christ* the Lord); boldly in John 4:26 (To the Samaritan woman who says she knows that the *Messiah* is coming, Jesus gives the forthright reply, 'I am he'); and then overwhelmingly in the pages of Acts and Paul, where Jesus is so often called Jesus *Christ* that the title has almost become a surname – 26 times in Acts, and 370 times in Paul.

But then, of course, we again have to ask the question (as we did for the title 'Son of God') whether Jesus himself ever accepted this title. Certainly, as we have seen above (p. 21), when Peter is asked by Jesus, 'Who do you think I am?' and replies, 'You are the *Christ*, the Son of God', Jesus replies, 'You are *not* to use that word about me!' And he says exactly the same in court, as we saw on the same page. Asked whether he is the *Christ*, the Son of God, he replies (at least on Matthew's account), 'That's *your* word, not mine!'

Many scholars appeal here to what is known as the 'Messianic Secret'. The popular understanding of the hoped-for Messiah had such political overtones, and evoked an image of salvation so alien to what Jesus had in mind, that even though he did claim to be the fulfilment of Israel's messianic hopes, he had to be secretive and avoid the word until the last moment, for fear of misunderstanding. But Messiah is what he claimed to be, as was very clear to the Romans who crucified him under the placard INRI – 'Jesus of Nazareth, *King* of the Jews'.

But there are many other scholars who have concluded that Jesus never claimed the title for himself at all. His followers, certainly, were unanimous in giving him this title, as if to say, 'Whatever else you were expecting, this is how God fulfilled those Old Testament promises and hopes, and this is all you're going to get'. But Jesus himself, as a good Jew, would have agreed with his fellow countrymen that what he stood for was something very different from the

Old Testament hopes of a Messiah. There are other ways in which the Old Testament expressed its hopes for God to bring his creation to its final fulfilment, in which a Messiah plays no part – the Restoration of Paradise, or the Completion of the Exodus into the True Promised Land, or the Coming of God to dwell in the midst of his People, or the New Creation, etc. You don't have to believe in a Messiah to be a good Jew. And Jesus was a good Jew.

Questions for Discussion

- In New Testament times, *all* Jews prayed and longed for the coming of the 'Messiah-Christ'. This is no longer the case for Jews, let alone for the Gentile world. Has the title become useless?

- Are those Jews who no longer hope for *a* Messiah being unfaithful to their Scriptures?

3. SUFFERING SERVANT

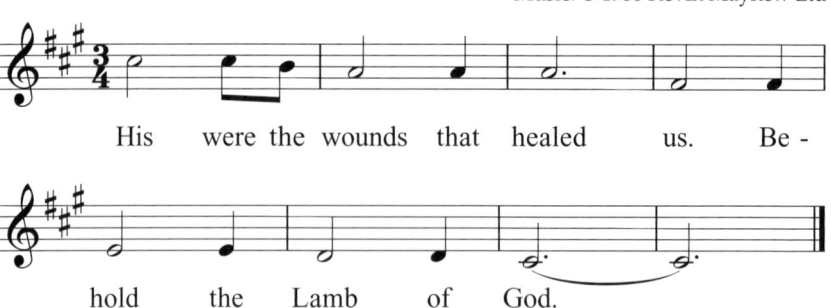

Text: H. J. Richards
Music: © 1986 Kevin Mayhew Ltd

His were the wounds that healed us. Behold the Lamb of God.

Towards the end of the Book of Isaiah, there are four related poems which have been given the name 'Songs of the Suffering Servant'. They describe the true Servant of God who is given a task which will make him suffer bitterly, but who finally comes to the understanding that his suffering – and even his death – will win the conversion of the world, and his own vindication (Isaiah 52:13- 53:12). The songs have become famous in their Authorised Version wording through the music of Handel:

> He was despised and rejected,
> a man of sorrows and acquainted with grief . . .
> All we like sheep have gone astray,
> and the Lord has laid on him
> the iniquity of us all.

I don't think I have ever heard these words read out so effectively as when I was sharing a platform with a Jewish rabbi, who was going to give a commentary on them. In the middle of reading one of the poems, he suddenly stopped, and there was dead silence for rather longer than is usually required for an oratorical pause. I looked up. He was choked with tears and couldn't go on. There were we, his Christian audience, merrily borrowing these words to apply them to the Crucifixion, and we had heard them so often that they didn't disturb us at all. And there was he, knowing that these words were originally written about the persecuted Jews in the Exile of 500 BC, and the thought of that persecution continuing for century after century just overwhelmed him.

The early Christians saw this persecution of the Jews epitomised in one Jew – Jesus. That is why the New Testament does not hesitate to borrow these Old Testament words to describe him. This is done quite explicitly in Matthew 12:18ff:

> Here is my Servant, whom I have chosen, my Beloved, the Favourite of my soul. (Isaiah 42:1ff.)

But there are many other echoes of the Servant Songs elsewhere in the New Testament. For example:

> He took on himself our infirmities, and bore our sickness. (Matthew 8:17, cf. Isaiah 53:4)

> He was numbered among the criminals and transgressors. (Luke 22:37, cf. Isaiah 53:12)

> He was led like a lamb to the slaughter, and like a lamb he was dumb before his shearers. (Acts 8:32, cf. Isaiah 53:7)

> He did no wrong, he told no lie, he was silent under the rod; they cursed him and he kept his peace, he put his trust in God . . . All we like sheep had gone astray, till he led us back to God. His were the wounds that healed us. Behold the Lamb of God. (1 Peter 2:22-25, cf. Isaiah 53:5-9)

'Lamb of God', of course, is the title used by John the Baptist to greet Jesus at the beginning of his ministry. It has often been asked why a lamb should be described as being 'of God'. Is it not likely that this is another reference to the Isaiah songs, of the Servant of God who became a sacrificial lamb?

To what extent did Jesus himself identify with this title, so beloved by the early Christians? Perhaps some clue is given by the words put into his mouth by Mark and Luke:

> I have come, not to be served, but to be a *Servant*, and to give my life as a ransom for the many. (Mark 10:45, cf. Isaiah 53:4)

> Was it not ordained that the Christ should *suffer*, and so enter into glory? (Luke 24:26)

Many scholars regard it as quite possible that these poems of Isaiah inspired Jesus to take up the kind of ministry he did, seeing in them a blueprint for fulfilling the vocation of the whole of his people Israel. With the inference, of course, that the New Israel he hoped to found would demand precisely the same kind of self-sacrifice.

Questions for discussion

- Of the titles we give to Jesus, 'Suffering Servant of God' is the complete antithesis of the title 'God'. How do you reconcile the two?

- Who should be more surprised, Christians when they hear Jews applying the Suffering Servant Songs to themselves, or Jews when they hear Christians applying them to Jesus?

4. SAVIOUR

Text: Ascribed to Pope John XXII
Music: W. J. Maher

Soul of my Sa-viour, sanc-ti-fy my breast.

What does it mean when the New Testament calls Jesus 'Saviour'? As, for example, the angels in the nativity scene:

This day, in the city of David, a Saviour is born (Luke 2:11),

or the Samaritans at Jacob's Well:

This is the Saviour of the world (John 4:42),

or Peter before the Sanhedrim, or Paul preaching in the synagogue:

God has raised up Jesus as Leader and Saviour (Acts 5:31, 13:23),

or, over and over again, in the latest writings of the New Testament, at a time when the Romans had made a cult of their emperor as 'Salvator', and Christians felt the need to insist that the title belonged to Jesus, not Domitian or Nerva or Trajan.

What are these texts trying to say about Jesus? The name, like all the titles given to Jesus, is a metaphor, based on the common human experience of a need to be saved or rescued or extricated from the many and various predicaments that human beings get into – ignorance, danger, suffering, enslavement, perplexity, despair, ruin, sin . . . A Saviour is someone who brings liberation, safety, freedom, life . . .

In the Old Testament, Moses figures as a high-profile Saviour. So does the successor of Moses who completed his work of deliverance, Joshua; his name actually *means* 'Saviour' and is the name that would eventually be given to Jeshua of Nazareth. Many of Israel's Judges and Kings were similarly described as saviour of their people.

But the person to whom the Bible most frequently gives the title is God himself:

> My soul magnifies the Lord, and my spirit rejoices in God my Saviour. (Luke 1:47)

The Book of Isaiah (his Hebrew name *Yeshayahu* means 'God alone is Saviour') presents God as saying:

> Beside me there is *no* Saviour (Isaiah 43:11, 45:21; see Hosea 13:4).

God is the one who rescues the human race from its own self-destruction.

To the extent that the New Testament sees Jesus as the spit image of God, he is often referred to in its pages as 'Saviour', as we have seen above. The whole of his ministry consists of saving people – from sickness, from meaninglessness, from alienation from God and from each other, from death. What Jesus does is what God is always doing.

But of course that is a task which ordinary human beings are also called to do. The word 'Saviour', like so many of the titles we give to Jesus, is both a divine word and an utterly human one. It is perfectly correct to say, 'It's all in the hands of God', as long as we remember that *we* are the hands of God.

Questions for discussion

- In Llanguth's book *Jesus Christs* (1968) Jesus tells a stooped figure passing him on the road, 'I have come to save you from your sins.' 'And what should *I* save people from?' the old man asks. Can you suggest an answer?

- If Jesus' death saved the human race (and especially his followers) from sin and death, why do sin and death continue as merrily in AD as in BC, not least for his followers?

5. HOLY ONE OF GOD

Text: the Roman Missal. Music by Franz Schubert

Ho - ly, ho - ly, ho - ly Lord.

In Hebrew, the basic meaning of the word 'holiness' is 'separateness'. The 'holy' is that which is hived off from the ordinary, the worldly, the profane. 'Holy' means sacred, consecrated, awesome, *other*, and so beyond our grasp that it is fearful, terrifying even. When you meet the holy, you don't say, 'Isn't that sweet!' Quite the opposite: you cower and hide your face, begging it to go away!

God is *the* Holy One. The Old Testament frequently refers to him as 'The Holy One of Israel'. But insofar as his people are related to such a God, dedicated to him, consecrated to him, tied to him, they too are committed to be separate, different:

> You (Israel) must be holy, because Yahweh your God is holy. (Leviticus 19:2)

As we have seen already a number of times, the New Testament often gives to Jesus the titles which were originally designed for Israel. Jesus is the True Israel, fulfilling in his person what all God's people were called to do and to be. And so we have statements like that of Gabriel to Mary:

> Your child will be called holy (Luke 1:35),

or of the demoniacs cowering before Jesus:

> I know who you are, the Holy One of God (Luke 4:34),

or of Peter to Jesus when the crowds abandon him:

Who would we go to? You are the Holy One of God (John 6:69),

or again of Peter, now to the Jews praying at the Temple:

It was you who sentenced the Holy One to death (Acts 3:14).

But once again, we should not imagine that the title is reserved for Jesus alone. It's a name that can be given to everyone who shares in God's life – Christian, Jewish, Muslim or whatever. We are *all* called holy, saints, those who are different and somehow separate.

This is no easy vocation. How can anyone be at the same time both *in* the world, and yet not *of* it? The New Testament recognises the anomaly when it both commands Christians not to love the world (1 John 2:13) and reminds them that God so loved the world that he gave up his Son on its behalf (John 3:16). It suggests that godly people are called to practise an extraordinary combination of detachment and concern, in what Alec Vidler referred to as a 'holy worldliness'. They will care less for the world, and at the same time care more for it than the ungodly. They won't lose their heart to it, but may very well lose their life for it.

We seldom get the balance right. We are often so identified with the world that we cannot speak to it, and at other times so remote from it that again we are unable to speak to it. To practise holy worldliness means to walk on a constant knife edge. We fall off it when we are either too worldly or too other-worldly. In neither case are we practising holiness.

Questions for discussion

- It is said that 'the holy' is something which both attracts and repels, both delights and dismays. What does it do for you?

- To which extreme do you tend – concern for the world, or detachment from it?

6. CHOSEN – ELECT

Text and music: Lynn DeShazo and Martin J. Nystrom
© 1990 Integrity's Hosanna! Music

We are a cho - sen race.

'The Chosen One' or 'the Elect' is another title of Israel which was eventually conferred on Jesus. Israel always saw itself as having been selected, graciously chosen out from among all the nations. The Israelite people were God's intimates, his darlings, the Chosen Race. And such a choice brought with it, of course, not only privileges, but also responsibilities. Tevye's complaint in *Fiddler on the Roof* catches the ambiguity:

> Dear Lord, I know we are your Chosen People, but couldn't you now and again choose someone else?

In the course of Old Testament history, it became clear to the prophets that the title belonged properly only to those who lived up to the responsibilities it entailed. Famously:

> You alone have I known of all peoples in the world; and therefore you will be the first to be punished for your sins. (Amos 3:2)

In other words, only the True Israel, the remnant at the heart of Judaism, could strictly speaking be called the Chosen One. And the suggestion is frequently made that this remnant would dwindle to smaller and smaller numbers.

The New Testament claims that the title was eventually fully realised in one person only – Jesus. It is he who has to head the new community of the elect. So, at his baptism:

> This is my Son, *the* Chosen One (Luke 9:35),

and at his crucifixion:

> Let him save himself, if he *is* the Chosen One. (Luke 23:35)

Yet the community which he heads also share his title. As Peter puts it in his Epistle:

> You, the Christian community, are the Chosen Race, the Royal Priesthood. (1 Peter 2:9)

Questions for discussion

- Being chosen is both a privilege and a responsibility. Of which are you most aware in your chosenness?

- Does the consciousness of being chosen entitle anyone to regard others as unchosen?

7. MEDIATOR

Text: Charles Wesley
Music adapted from Mendelssohn by W. H. Cummings

Peace on earth and mercy mild, God and sinners reconciled.

The metaphor of 'mediation' is based on the ordinary everyday need for someone to mediate between two disaffected parties, to stand between them (Latin *medium*), to act as a go-between, able to speak on behalf of both sides, understanding and representing the interests of each.

In the Old Testament, Moses stands out as the model mediator, pleading Israel's case before God:

I alone stood between Yahweh and yourselves,

he claims in Deuteronomy 5:5, echoing his earlier scene in Exodus 17:11, where he is seated on a hillside watching Israel's battle with the Amalekites, his praying arms supported by Hur and Aaron, until they got so tired that they had to be replaced by two enormous rocks.

Priests in the Old Testament were also regarded as intermediaries, taking Israel's prayers to God, and God's answer back. Kings too fulfilled this role, being themselves seen as priestly figures standing between their people and God. Prophets as well, in their capacity of relaying God's messages to their people. And, among the prophets the Suffering Servant who, as we have seen, has become so identified with his people that he carries their sufferings.

The New Testament calls Jesus *the* Mediator par excellence. The strongest text is 1 Timothy 2:5:

> There is only one God, and only one Mediator between God and the human race, the man Jesus Christ,

but there are many other texts in the same vein, such as:

> In Christ, God was reconciling the world to himself, and the good news is that we are now reconciled (2 Corinthians 5:19).

The term is most often used in the Epistle to the Hebrews, with its overpowering emphasis on the metaphor of priesthood. Here Jesus is presented as the epitome of the Jewish priesthood. He is the great High Priest, the mediator of a New and better Covenant. He alone, of all the human race, enters the Sanctuary of God (a privilege reserved for the High Priest) and we follow in his wake (see Hebrews 8:6, 12:24, etc.).

As Mediator, then, it is Jesus' humanity that is being stressed, rather than his divinity. The Epistle is anxious to point this out over and over again:

> He did not appoint angels to be rulers of the world to come, but a man. (2:5-9)

> The one who sanctifies and the ones who are sanctified are of the same stock; that is why he openly calls them brothers. (2:11-12)

> He was totally identified with his brothers, a compassionate high priest of God's religion. (2:17)

> It is not as if we had a high priest who was incapable of feeling our weaknesses with us; we have one who has been tempted in every way that we are. (4:15)

> He can sympathise with those who are ignorant or uncertain, because he too lives in the limitations of weakness. (5:2)

Although he was Son, he had to learn to obey through suffering. (5:8)

Questions for discussion

- To what extent do you regard Jesus as your spokesman before God?

- When mediation is needed between two disaffected parties, do you rush in, or retire quickly?

8. PROPHET

Text: Edwin Hatch
Music: Charles Lockhart

Breathe on me, breath of God.

The Hebrew word for prophet (*nabi*) means 'ecstatic', and that is what the earliest Israelite prophets were. But in the course of their history, they settled down to something less wild (though no less dangerous), as spokesmen or mouthpieces for God – which is the meaning of the Greek word *prophetes*. They were seen as people into whom God breathed (hence the word 'inspiration'), so that what emerged from their mouths was no longer their own words, but the Word of God (see Section One, Chapter 3).

Deuteronomy 18 presents Moses as the model mouthpiece for God, and promises that when Moses dies, God will provide another to continue his work. In the context, this is clearly a reference to the whole institution of prophetism. But the text is ambiguous enough to suggest a single future spokesman for God, another Moses. And this is how the text was eventually interpreted, especially towards the end of the Old Testament, when the attempts to restore the monarchy had failed again and again, and Jewish hopes for a New David (Messiah-Christ) were abandoned in favour of a New Moses.

The New Testament claims that this hope (like all the others we have considered above) was fulfilled in Jesus:

'He shall be called *the* Prophet of the Most High'

announces the angel to Mary (Luke 1:76). People ask John the Baptist:

Are you *the* prophet? –

and they are told to look over the horizon to the approaching Jesus (John 1:21). After the meal in the desert, people ask:

Is this *the* Prophet who is to come? (John 6:14),

and the question is repeated in the following chapter. (John 7:40)

And in his address to the crowd gathered at the Jerusalem Temple, Peter quotes the Deuteronomy text referred to above, of a new Moses to come, and explicitly interprets it as having been fulfilled in Jesus. (Acts 3:22)

Jesus as 'the Prophet' ties in, of course, with what was said above in Chapter 3 about Jesus as the Word of God. Not that the prophets ever claimed to *be* the Words of God; it was only their message that they claimed to have divine authority. But their office in the story of the Old Testament was in the long run so influential that all the sacred writings attributed to Moses and his prophetic successors were regarded as the Word of God. It is this aspect which links them with Jesus, who is said not only to have preached the Word of God but also to have embodied it in his whole life and death.

The New Testament presumes that the office of prophetism is continued in the disciples of Jesus the Prophet. Peter proudly announces on the first Pentecost Day that the wild Old Testament hope for a time when all men and women would be filled with God's Spirit and proclaim God's Word was now fulfilled. Every Christian is called upon to bear prophetic witness to what God has done in Christ.

Questions for discussion

- To what extent can the Church be said to continue the prophetic role of Jesus?

- What aspect of your life bears the best prophetic witness to the Gospel? And the worst?

9. SECOND ADAM – IMAGE OF GOD

Text: John Henry Newman
Music: Richard Runciman Terry. © Burns & Oates Ltd

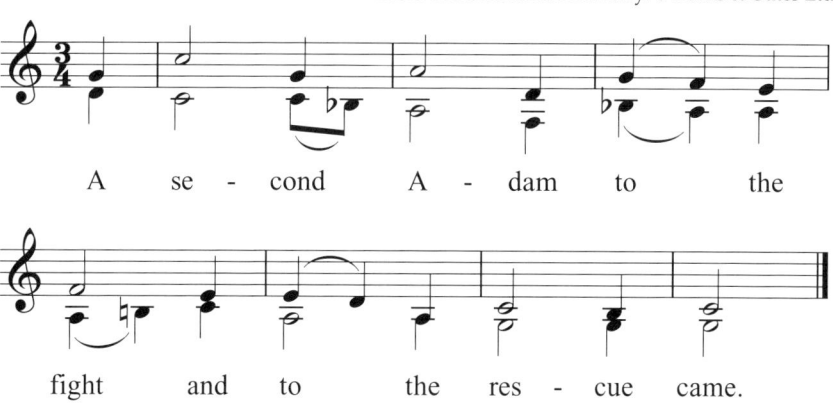

A second Adam to the fight and to the rescue came.

This name has already been touched on in Section Two, Chapter 1 under the title Son of Man (Hebrew *Ben Adam*). But in this instance Jesus is not simply like the rest of his brothers a son of Adam – he is *another* Adam, the beginning of a new human race.

We find the title, explicitly or implied, in texts like:

Sin entered the world through the one man Adam,
and he prefigured the one man Jesus Christ,
through whom salvation has entered the world. (Romans 5:12ff.)

Christ is the template for all his followers, just as Adam (made in the image of God) was God's prototype for the whole human race. (see Romans 8:29)

As in Adam (climax of the First Creation) all die,
so will all brought to life in Christ,
(the beginning of a New Creation). (1 Corinthians 15:22)

> Christ was the very image of God,
> and he showed this by becoming a servant,
> unlike Adam who tried to become God's equal. (see Philippians 2:11ff.)
>
> Christ is the New Man, created by God. (see Ephesians 2:15)
>
> Christ is the New Adam, the Second Adam, the beginning of a new creation. (see 1 Corinthians 15:45ff.)

I find texts like these very reassuring, after the heavy insistence of Jesus' divinity in some of the texts referred to earlier. In Hebrew, the word 'Adam' means quite simply 'man'. This implies that the story of Adam on the opening pages of the Bible is not to be taken as the *history* of an individual standing at the beginning of all things, but as an allegory about the whole of human kind.

And what does it say about Adam (meaning all of us?). That we are totally dependent on the God who created us. That in spite of this we are the Lords of creation, in which we stand as the very image of God, mirroring God's own life and creativity. And that we stand in the midst of our fellow creatures as a kind of embodiment of God, not needing to discard our humble humanity, or even to transcend it, in order to make the invisible God visible.

Christians are those who claim that the member of the human race who has done that to perfection is the man Jesus, and that in him a new human race has begun to people the earth. Preposterous or what?

Questions for discussion

- The community founded by Jesus, the new Adam, claims to be the nucleus of a new Creation. How credible is this claim?

- As an Adam or Eve of today, to what extent do you mirror God's own life and creativity?

15. CONCLUSION

Who was Jesus? Who did *he* think he was?

Did he think he was what people *said* he was?

Jesus was, just like the rest of us, a child of God, a son of God. But such a Son that he revealed God to us in a way no other son or daughter has done, before or since. He embodied perfectly the maxim 'Like father like son'. He was the spit image of his Father. To see him was to see God, insofar as the totally invisible God *can* be seen.

It is for this reason that we have given him the titles which express as best we can that once-for-all character that we have found in this man:

> He is the Word of God, the Truth about God, not distorted in the way we constantly distort it.
>
> He is the Way to God – though others have found other ways.
>
> He is the very Reflection of God in earthly terms.
>
> He is someone in whom God (in the sky?) has come *down* to us.
>
> He is someone in whom God (Ground of Being?) has come *through* to us.

None of these descriptions or titles removes Jesus from the human race.

People used to read the Gospels quite uncritically, as if they were blow-by-blow accounts of what happened, based on diaries kept by Matthew, Mark, Luke and John. Scholars today are more critical. They agree that the Gospels stand on a very sound basis – they are not fairy stories – but they have concluded that it would be more accurate to read them as frankly confessional documents. That is to say, the writers do not pretend to present who Jesus *was* in the years 0 to 30 AD. They quite openly set out to tell their readers in the years 60 to 100 AD who Jesus *is*, and what Jesus *means* to them.

Let's put that the other way round. On the one hand, it is quite clear that the Jesus of History does actually stand behind the Gospel stories about him. On the other hand, it is also clear that the Christ of Faith has been superimposed on those stories, and that what we are looking at now is a double image. If readers of the Gospel do not allow for this, they are in danger of getting a very distorted picture.

To help my students understand this, I have told them that the Gospels are like a wine. For those who are unaware of it, wine is actually made from real grapes! But you can't deconstruct the wine back into grapes. And who would want to, anyway?

It could be objected that this leaves the Gospel writers open to a charge of falsification. The answer is that it is exactly the other way round! If the evangelists had only told us what Jesus meant to his disciples back then, *that* would be the falsification. What they are actually saying is, 'This is what Jesus means to us *now*, now that we have seen his life in perspective, now that the penny has dropped.' What they are actually saying is, 'Does he mean the same to you?'

Most of the studies of Jesus (Christologies) that have been made in the past have been based on a biographical reading of the Gospels. What such studies have produced, inevitably, has been a hybrid Jesus, half human and half divine. What the Christian faith commits us to, however, is a conviction that Jesus was *totally* human. If any of the titles that we give him obscure that conviction (worse still, sometimes even obliterate that conviction), then we must rethink all our categories. Which is what I have tried to do in the chapters above.

It must be asked in conclusion how all that has been said on these pages tie in with our traditional profession of faith, in which God is not just 'God, full stop', but a Trinity of Father, Son and Holy Spirit. A fair question. Let me try to give a fair answer.

The Hebrew Bible speaks neither of a Trinity, nor of a God different from the God of the Gospels. It speaks unswervingly of a

CONCLUSION

Father, who alone creates, teaches, liberates, loves and dwells with his people Israel, whom he calls to become his Son.

The Gospels present Jesus as this true Israel, who recognises God as his 'Father', and shows the world what it means to be the *Son* of such a God, most clearly in his death.

After his death, Jesus lives on in those who live as he did, and who show themselves to be possessed by the same *Spirit* of sonship that characterised his life.

In short, the reality to which people give the name 'God' is an unfathomable mystery, so far beyond human reach that, if he didn't breathe a word, no one would ever know anything about him. Christians acknowledge that there has never been a time when God did not breathe a word: he has always made himself known. But, they claim, the Word of God was never breathed more clearly than in the life and death of *Jesus*. And that Breath (or *Spirit*) is still felt in the inspiration that Jesus is able to give, even after his death.

Christians claim to know the *Father* through the *Spirit* of *Jesus*. That is what the word 'Trinity' is trying to express. Trinity means that the one *God* can best be found in the life and teaching of the man Jesus, who was so filled with God's *Spirit* that (like father like son) he can be called the *Son* of God. His followers are those who feel themselves inspired by the same Spirit, and know that when they live as he did, and make his values their own, they will be at one with God as he was.

For discussion

- This short explanation of the relationship between Father, Son and Holy Spirit may be more understandable for many who are flummoxed by official Trinitarian Theology. Does that make it suspect?

Acknowledgements

The publishers wish to express their gratitude to the following for permission to include copyright material in this book:

Burns & Oates Ltd, Wellwood, North Farm Road, Tunbridge Wells, Kent, TN2 3QR, UK, for the Music *'Billing'* by R. R. Terry.

Kingsway's Thankyou Music, P.O. Box 75, Eastbourne, East Sussex, BN23 6NW, UK, for the extracts from *'You have called us'* by Lynn De Shazo and Martin J. Nystrom. © 1990 Integrity's Hosanna! Music. (For the UK only.)